Change One

Live Your Life
Without Fear

Other Books by R and R

Meditation for beginners
What is Meditation, and how can it change your life?
A Guide to mindfulness and happiness.

F*ck Motivation
It's your life. A guide on how to live your life and be happy.

Declutter
A beginners 10 step guide on how to simplify life by decluttering.

New Habits - New Wealth
How changing some habits can improve your personal health and financial wealth.

Puppy Training
Top 10 ideas for training your dog within a month to keep everybody in your house happy and stress-free.

Minimalist
The How-To and Why of becoming a minimalist

www.randrdigitallifestyle.com

licensed professional before attempting any techniques outlined in this book.

By reading this document, the reader agrees that under no circumstances are the authors responsible for any losses, direct or indirect, which are incurred as a result of the use of information contained within this document, including, but not limited to, —errors, omissions, or inaccuracies.

Table of Contents

Introduction

It's Monday. Again.

You already know what's going to happen before you even get out of bed. It's breakfast, it's the commute, it's the office, it's the *boss,* it's life. Just like last week. And the week before. You stay under the covers for just a few moments longer, relishing the peaceful silence before the hectic chaos of the workday begins. The sun is coming up over the horizon, just peeking through the crack in the curtains, slicing through the darkness to open up this sweet retreat to the world beyond. Birds are singing joyfully outside the window, blissfully oblivious to the drudgery and toil that awaits you. Out there. At work.

It didn't always use to be like this. Did it? No, you can remember a different time, a better time. When morning meant a new opportunity, a new challenge, a new adventure, a new chance at greatness. The problem is, you haven't felt like that in some time. Now the sweetest part of the day isn't getting up to face the world, but finally laying down at night to escape it.

We're here to help.

There is an epidemic facing humankind today, and it has been plaguing us since the dawn of time. It isn't a killer parasite or incapacitating virus, but a silent killer. Not of men, but of dreams. It is fear.

Where does this fear come from? Is it natural? Is it internal, or external? Can it be defeated, finally conquered? Do we fight it, or embrace it? These are some of the questions that we plan on answering as we tackle fear head-on, shining a light on the boogeyman in the dark and exposing fear for what it really is: a dream killer.

"Change One Thing – <u>Understand</u> your fears!

Chapter One: The Destination

Where to?

Fear is nothing. Really. Fear is nothing. Nothing. The fear that we experience is real, don't get it wrong, but it doesn't have to be a real obstacle. You have dreams, and you can accomplish them. What's stopping you? What we want to do is help you achieve any goal you set your mind to, and the first step is to actually set your mind to it. *"Change One Thing – Set your mind on where you want to go."* Fear of the unknown is enough to stop most people in their tracks, but it doesn't have to stop you. The unknown is nothing to be afraid of. The unknown is an opportunity waiting to be taken advantage of. There are several things we can do to cope with the fear in our lives, particularly the fear of the unknown, the fear of change. The first, and most important, is to reduce the number of unknowns. If uncertainty is a source of fear, then we should be ready to take drastic measures to increase our level of certainty. This all starts with recognizing just how much we can know beforehand.

Life, as they say, is a journey. The question isn't where are you going, or even necessarily, how are you getting there. The question is, are you going where you want to be going? We are all here journeying together, traveling the road set before us as best we can, diligently striving forward toward the destination. But where is that? If you're like most of us, chances are excellent that at some point, without even realizing it, you've switched routes, heading for a destination that you didn't ever see coming.

It's not always easy to distinguish if we are off the path or not, sometimes diverging roads can appear very similar from our point of view. We stand close to the road, sometimes caught up in the passing scenery and traffic around us, too busy or distracted to ever look further ahead. Step back, don't take a closer look, take a further look. See yourself from 1000 feet up and ask, 'where does this road lead?' It is common for people to say that it's not the destination that matters, but the journey. This is the reprieve of those who either can't see their destination or those who can and know already it's not worth the trip.

We've all been lost at least once, somewhere, and it's not a good feeling. Your heart sinks as you realize that the direction you were confidently traveling has proven erroneous, your efforts not only unproductive but actually, counter-productive-you've been going in the wrong direction! Take heart, you are not alone. Perhaps you've found yourself in a dead-end job that just seems to lead nowhere, a never-ending cycle of stress, trading time for money, at an exchange rate that's just never in your favor. Or maybe you've been one of the fortunate ones, who actually managed to mark out a career for yourself, something you love, something you're proud of. Now, retirement looms, you're not getting any younger, and that business is no closer to running itself than the day you started it. Maybe you just can't give up that paycheck yet and still live comfortably.

Regardless of where you find yourself on life's journey, don't let yourself get upset about where you are. Instead, we're going to focus on where you're going. Where you *want* to go. In order to make any significant changes in our lives, we have to be able to start by making little changes. Every war begins with a single gunshot, and we all know you can only eat an elephant one bite at a time. Changes are going to come in steps, and the first step is identifying where you actually want to go. The fear we experience when it comes to contemplating the unknown is not actually rational. The underlying emotions we feel when considering significant life changes seem like fear of the unknown, but this is actually a mischaracterization. The unknown isn't what is scary to us, but rather the prospect of losing what we do know. Those may sound like different ways of saying the same thing but are, in fact, quite different.

Losing the known comforts that we currently enjoy is the real root of the fear we have about making significant changes. The irrationality of it lies in this: if what we were presently clinging to in fear and desperation was so valuable, why are we then contemplating such dramatic changes, unless we actually desire something much better? It is perfectly rational to feel a real attachment to those foundational underpinnings of our lives, like a job, housing, or connections to a community. What must be remembered is that we don't simply give up those things we hold dear and jump into the great unknown. The prospect of any positive life change you may be considering is that you gain something you didn't have before, something that you deem more valuable than your current circumstances. If you desire to get out of miserable winters and finally move to a southern state, the fear is not really whether you'd be happy in the sunshine, it's about if you can be happy without your current home. Just remember the reason for the trade-off.

This should be a time for you to really sit down and evaluate things, take stock of what you are doing in life, and make sober decisions about where you want to be. Approaching major life changes with a Pollyanna attitude and with statements like 'I see myself winning the lottery' aren't going to help at all. Make a list. This is the big picture, the 10,000-foot view of your life, and what you want to achieve. It could be retirement, starting a business, staying home to have kids, going back to school, moving for a new job, you name it. You need to be able to see your life, not as a series of disjointed occurrences and unrelated decisions, but as a continuous whole, a closely interrelated mosaic of choices, each one in some way leading on towards a common goal.

Let's start with an analogy. Imagine ants. Lots of them. One giant anthill, teeming with life, and what we see above ground is literally only the tip of the network. There is a vast underground labyrinth of tunnels and chambers, the ants all busy about their work, day in and day out. Now, there are different ants for different jobs; some gather food, others build and repair the tunnels, and of course, there is the queen. All of these ants, regardless of the task before them, are all working towards a common goal. If you could stop any ant at any time and ask her what she's doing, she would always respond the same: serving the colony. So must our life be organized, so that every decision, every opportunity, every action we take, is geared towards that one, over-arching goal of our life. Is it saving money for retirement? Then surely you won't be caught splurging on that old hot rod you saw for sale, right? At the risk of redundancy, the first step to achieving your goals is going to be actually *making* them your goals. We can't take the first step of our journey until we know the destination.

"Change One Thing – <u>Decide</u> where you want to go!"

Chapter Two: The Route

Making a list

We've shown you that the fear that may be holding you back from what you really want is actually an irrational fear. When considered logically, the prospect of postponing your dreams in order to secure a more firm grip on a reality that doesn't actually serve your purposes is counterproductive. Once we establish that there is a life you can work to achieve that would fulfill more of your wants and needs than your current life, what could possibly be the motivation for hanging on to what you have? Nonetheless, we fully recognize that the fear, though irrational, remains. This is part of the human condition; if we were capable of only doing and thinking those things that are rational, we would be robots, not people.

This doesn't mean you can't still control this fear, subdue it, and use it to your advantage. First of all, fear can be a great motivator, but we must understand in what direction it drives us, and to what ends. In this case, the best approach to overcoming these fears is to attempt to plan them out of existence. Where knowledge abounds, fear is absent. So, let's look at what we know.

Just like in any other journey, you're probably going to find out that there are multiple ways to reach your destination, all with their own unique features. Let's take the example of starting a restaurant. For somebody who doesn't have a lot of experience in running that sort of business, starting out can be very daunting. Many different things need to happen for the final goal to be realized. What you need to do is start breaking this down, one step at a time in order to lay out the route that is best going to suit your needs, as well as your desires.

Starting a restaurant could be reduced to a few substantial steps, for example:

Get a loan to buy an existing restaurant business

Hire staff

Set menu

Open

This is much too general of a list for 99% of people with this goal. Perhaps if you had opened 30 other restaurants already, it would be this simple for you, but there is more to it than this. Not only is our list of steps going to have more content, but it will also have options as well. Let's see an example of how that may look:

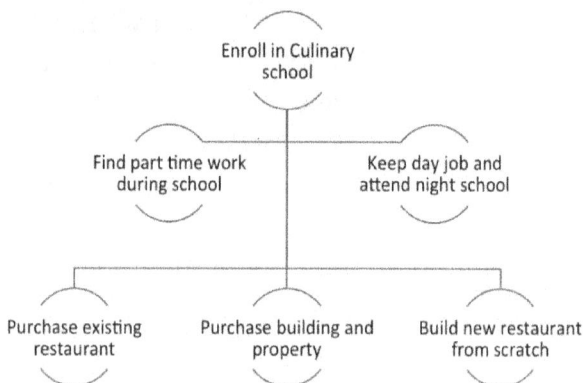

Here we've identified just the first few major steps of the plan, and already we have some decisions to make about what route we want to take to reach our destination. Whether we spend 2+ years getting culinary training or not will have a significant impact on the accomplishment of our goals. You would have a solid foundation of necessary skills that will undoubtedly help you achieve your dreams, but it requires a considerable investment of both time and money just to get your feet off the ground. This decision, however, not only affects the timeline of achieving your goal, it directly affects the quality of the outcome. In this case, you could forego any training and rely on hired help to assist you with the details. This would be a feasible path to take, but you would be taking part of the responsibility of reaching your goals and putting it on someone else's shoulders. We can't achieve any goals entirely on our own, but with relevant technical training, you would be much better equipped to realize your goal in the long run.

Additionally, there are several ways to acquire a building. Designing from the ground up is a big undertaking that allows you to make the restaurant represent your vision precisely. Usually unforeseen by potential builders are the shortcomings of new construction, such as missed deadlines by contractors, incorrect or unavailable materials, even weather can play a significant role. Purchasing a functional restaurant takes most of the guesswork out of what you'll need to get started, but you'll have someone else's history of problems and decisions to contend with. Budget restrictions will apply to both choices, determining how much of your vision you can actually afford. Ultimately, what's going to determine which route you lay out for yourself is knowing what choices are most in line with your desires.

Taking the time to make a list, step by step, of everything you would need to do to accomplish your goals is critical. This is how we take the fear of change and turn it into a force for good, by allowing it to motivate us to positive action. There is an interesting practice among Japanese businesses when it comes to planning the future of companies. In Japan, it has long been a traditional characteristic of the people as a whole to consider things on a much greater time scale than what we're used to in America. Our country has been around for a couple hundred years, theirs for millennia. In business, Japanese companies often write out business plans that specify goals for the company 100 years from now. That's right, 100 years. People sit down around conference tables and discuss where the company should be long after everyone in the room is dead. Now that's some long-term planning. The result of this is that the whole company takes on a different mindset, where the employees don't see it as just another job with a paycheck for this week, but that they are part of something much greater, that can last much longer if they all work towards the same goals.

Sit down and actually plan everything you can think of that would be involved in achieving the life goals you've set out. This is not a one-year plan or five-year plan, but a 'the rest of your life' plan. It may sound daunting, but this should not only be easy, but actually fun. After all, it's your life we're talking about here, what do you want it to look like? The more details we can fill in now, the greater the likelihood you'll actually reach each of those steps. Besides, detailed planning will help you to identify as many pitfalls as possible before they come along.

"Change One Thing – <u>Plan</u> where you want to go."

Chapter Three: Roadblocks

Many roadblocks may present themselves to you along your path, but the fear of them is what is going to turn them into major catastrophes, instead of small detours. When the fear of tripping up on a bump in the road is enough to prevent us from continuing on our journey, we've begun to see our problems as much more significant than they actually are.

The steps are in place for you to follow, and now you must access the path ahead for any roadblocks or hazards that may hinder your success. There are bound to be some pitfalls along the way that we just can't plan for, and this is not only part of any long-term planning process, but really part of life in general. Knowing that we will have some degree of calamity before us, we should be diligent in attending to any possible adverse circumstances that advance planning may alleviate.

Life's hurdles can be many and grievous, but planning ahead as best we are able can help us to overcome many of them in stride. Nothing comes easy, and if it does, it is likely not worth working for in the first place. The important thing to remember is that even insurmountable obstacles don't have to be deal breakers, they simply require a different path. Let's look at some examples of possible roadblocks that you may face, and investigate how some prudence and good judgment can help you succeed no matter what comes your way.

1. Money

This is the big one, the hazard that consumes more good planning than any other. So many people get tripped up by money, that they start to think that money is the actual problem, instead of a tool to be used for solving problems. When we let money become the driving force in our lives, the inevitable result is that we will never actually be able to achieve our goals, because the goal is, by definition, unachievable. To go to work each day with the purpose of having 'more money' is to set yourself up for failure before you even leave the house.

First of all, 'more money' is not a quantifiable metric, meaning we can't actually measure our success. How much more? A thousand dollars a month? A million dollars outright? What is the number you're going to put on this goal? Any time you set a goal without clear, defined limits you've given yourself a moving target that will change every time you look at it. The end result is that if you try and assess your progress, it will always appear as if you're falling short. We must be careful to define our goals, which is what the first part of the planning stage is for.

The other aspect of misrepresenting money this way is the presumption that money in itself is going to be a worthwhile goal. While money itself is, of course, harmless, the relentless pursuit of money can lead to some very unwanted consequences. We all have things we need more money for. It could be something rather straightforward, like a particular car, or a trip you've always wanted to take. It could also be a little more intangible, such as 'enough' money for retirement, or to travel the world for a year. In these circumstances it is appropriate, as much as is possible, to define an actual dollar amount, whether that be a set figure, like say $100,000, or a particular income, like an extra $500/month. These are useful ways to use money as a goal, but we must remember that it is not the ultimate goal, but simply one of the landmarks we must visit on the way to our final goal. The money will always be a tool, a means, but never an end in itself. After all, how much fun would you really have kicking back in your rocking chair on the porch, shuffling through a bag of cash? It would be entertaining for a minute or two, but is hardly the kind of long-lasting fulfillment that we're after. Besides, even if money could buy happiness, it could never actually *be* happiness.

Aside from the general relationship that we need to have with money in order to ensure long-term happiness and the successful pursuit of our dreams, we also need to be realistic when assessing just how much money it may take to achieve our goals. Often people are somewhat pie-in-the-sky about how things are going to turn out, literally relying on the power of positive thinking to sort out all the details for them. While we must not underestimate the potential of the human will to achieve remarkable things, it would be pure folly to rely on our positive outlook to pay the bills.

This is where a little research can go a long way toward not only helping us shape our plan of action but relieve any potential anxiety about the unknown. Maybe you always wanted to be a nurse, to be able to go to work every day and help people who are in need, truly making a difference in the lives of others. However, you found yourself on a different path in life, and now after many years, have a desire to go back to school for nursing, and finally realize the dream you've always wanted. Before you go too far, stop and investigate just what that might look like if you actually achieve it. Do you live near a hospital, or would you have to commute an hour? Private practice, or not? What is the average salary for a nurse anyway? Can you live as comfortably on a nurse's salary as you do right now? Do you need to? How much is the school going to cost? What would be the salary trade-off if you went to school for 4 years, instead of 2?

It is important not to let the financial side of things surprise you because you're likely to have enough surprises already. Perhaps instead of a new career, you're looking to retire and enjoy your golden years in ease and comfort. Well, how much money do you need to do that? Are your retirement savings going to last for the next 20 or more years? Will you need to work part-time to supplement that income in order to maintain the same quality of life that you enjoy now? Will you be one of the many people who retire only to find out that they don't have enough activities to fill their day anymore, and end up working just to keep busy? This may be an easy source of income that you weren't initially planning on.

2. Time

Everybody needs more time. It's simply a fact of life. The more we use, the less we have. What's worse, is when you let any slip through your fingers, you can never get it back. When it comes to planning for the future, our concept of time can be very misleading. When we're young, time seems to be that infinite resource, always there when we need it. Of course, as we get older reality starts to set in, and the days and weeks begin to fly by. We suddenly wonder where all the time went, and how so much of it was wasted on things that just don't seem to matter now.

When it comes to relieving our fears, few things are as beneficial as having a schedule. It is well known among childcare specialists that children thrive on routine. The more predictable, rote, and dependable a day is for a child, the better they can function and grow because the fear of not knowing what to expect has been removed for them. A child who lives in an unpredictable world, with lots of radical changes to mealtimes and bedtimes, will have great difficulty adjusting to their world because it is a moving target. Ultimately, the growth they will experience will be learning to adapt to change itself, rather than the world around them.

This same principle holds true in adulthood. Though we are capable of handling far more complicated and unpredictable circumstances than children, the reality is the same; we thrive the most when we know what to expect. Setting your life on a schedule will help you to make the most of the time that you have before you. We recognize every day is essential, and that there is almost no way to ever accomplish everything we would like to in the span of a mere 24 hours. Time management becomes a fundamental skill for life in general, and those who are poor at it will suffer the results of reduced productivity, and ultimately happiness. No less important is the planning of time on a long-term basis. As you begin to lay out the goals, which you would like to achieve, remember to give them dates. In fact, give them 2 dates.

The first date to give any goal is a due date. This will be the date you set for yourself to accomplish the goal. Let's say you have the goal of quitting your job and starting a home business. Once you've established the parameters by which you can determine if this goal is met (perhaps making 2/3 of your current income from the home business in order to quit your job) you then must set a due date. Don't be afraid of specificity, it will only add to the gravity of the accomplishment. Instead of setting a due date of the year 2023, decide on March 31, 2023. The more specific the time frame, the surer we are to work towards that date. When you say 'someday I would like to...' it has no weight at all, and takes the form of pure fantasy. This way of speaking about the future relegates it to the land of make-believe, a far-off distant dream world that may not ever come to fruition. Conversely, when you say 'this afternoon, I have a 3:00pm meeting' it couldn't be more concrete. There is no mistaking where you will be at 3:00pm. Likewise, you should treat your goals with the same respect. If we are diligent about outlining specific timelines for things like lunch, a trip to the grocery store, or a movie with friends, how much greater emphasis should we place on the timelines for fulfilling our greatest desires and biggest achievements in life?

The usual tendency is for people to assume goals that are far away must necessarily be vague, but this is not the case. When we see something with our eyes that is far away, it is harder to define the farther it is. However, when we see something with our mind's eye that is far off, we can use our reasoning powers to bring it into focus. Our physical limitations need not be our mental limitations. Fear and uncertainty can easily creep in around an undefined goal. Knowing precisely what the goal looks like is only part of the battle; it is crucial to define a timeline. Our planning will become even more powerful and effective when we lay out due dates for as many things as possible. Once you've set the steps in place to achieve a particular goal, setting due dates for each step will keep you accountable, productive, and help keep fear safely at bay.

The process of setting due dates is rather straightforward. Decide on a date for the final realization of the goal, and every other date for the remaining steps will fall into place behind it. For example, if your date to quit working full-time and focus on a home business is March 31, 2023, then you work backward from there to determine the steps before it. Here's how it may look:

Mar 31, 2023: Quit full-time job

Feb 28, 2023: Pass $3000/month in sales at home business

Jul 31, 2022: Have at least 10 products that sell $200/month each

Dec 31, 2021: Have 6 products officially launched

Jul 31, 2021: Have website fully functional and online

What this does is force you to evaluate how long it should take to accomplish each step, and in doing so allow you to set not just arbitrary dates, but realistic ones that you can work towards. Accountability increases as you hold yourself responsible not only for accomplishing the goals, but doing so within a specific, well-defined timeline.

The second date we should set for our goals is an expiration date. This may sound a little pessimistic, but we're not talking about gallons of milk that we throw away. Rather, an expiration date on a goal will allow you to evaluate if it is actually a worthy goal or not. The reason for this kind of date is not so we can discard lifelong dreams after missing a deadline, but so we can be assured that the dreams we are chasing are actually the ones that are going to make us happy.

Suppose the home business plan above is moving along, and after some time you've met a few goals, but now progress has started to stagnate, and you've missed a couple due dates. The expiration date you set for yourself is one month from the due date, or

April 30, 2023. Time marches on, and before you know it, you've reached the expiration date and are nowhere near ready to retire. The website is up and running, and you've generated some sales, but the stated steps haven't been met, and you're not in a position to quit your job by the expiration date. What happened?

Sure, this could be a case of poor diligence, you didn't spend enough time on the business, sales have been sluggish, and therefore the income has been insufficient to support you on a full-time basis. What if there's more to it than that? Perhaps a serious illness had you sidetracked for a couple months, and now you've fallen behind. If that's the case, then the setback is temporary, and you can adjust your dates accordingly to stay on track. But what if you haven't been putting the time into the business because you just don't actually enjoy it? Maybe it didn't turn out to be near as fulfilling as you had imagined, and instead of working on the business you've been spending more time trying to gig on the weekends with your friends in a band. The expiration date will force you to examine the goals and see if they still fit your desires. What seems like a great idea now may quickly need some tweaks 3 or 4 years from now. This would be an excellent opportunity to decide if maybe pursuing a music career isn't something that would be more satisfying and fulfilling than a home business, and yet still allow you to meet the same financial goals you initially set. In this case, we're able to achieve the same results we set out for, but take an entirely different path to get there.

The paradoxical aspect of a structured plan is that it actually allows for greater flexibility overall. When the important goals are known and fixed, like replacing your current income, the path you take to get there can take many different shapes, because you always have that focused, defined goal to guide your way.

3. Other people

Naturally, people cause problems. We create problems for ourselves, often times for others, and others will inevitably cause problems for us. Like all the other challenges you are going to face in life, this one can be minimized, worked around, prepared for, but never totally avoided.

One of the ways to know you are genuinely changing something significant in your life is to listen to what other people have to say about it. When things are plugging along like 'normal,' there aren't usually a lot of uninvited comments about our lives. When we start to upset the apple cart though, when we begin to rock the boat and make a few waves, this is when you can count on some free advice, and usually lots of it.

The most likely place you are going to find dissension will be within your own family. It can be very difficult for us to receive any criticism from our loved ones, especially when it comes to something important to us, such as chasing after a dream of ours that we never dared to do before. Sometimes this criticism can take a very negative form, and turn into outright insults and degradation. It's vital that you don't allow that kind of talk to slow down your progress towards your dreams. There may even be genuine care and compassion behind some comments that end up causing a great deal of hurt and pain, but if the only way someone can communicate their love for you is through hurtful, derogatory language, then you need to distance yourself from them as soon as possible. Any person in your life who truly has your best interests in mind would want you to be happy and healthy. So, if that same person prohibits you from enjoying those benefits, then they've argued themselves out of your social circle on their own.

Now we must be careful to differentiate between those who mean well and those who are just mean. It would be nice to say that all of our critiques would come out of a sincere heart from someone who loves us dearly, but often this is not the case, as we are all subject to the same human condition, and the same tendencies to bitterness, envy, and strife. There are essentially two types of negative people you must deal with in following the path to your dreams, those who hinder you intentionally, and those who do it unwittingly.

For the former category, the solution is plain, though the implementation can be radically difficult. To remove naysayers from our lives is easy to say, but very hard to do. Casual relationships with neighbors and friends may not be so important to you in the long run, and therefore, negative comments may be easily avoided by limiting contact with those people. Even working relationships can be worked around to avoid toxicity, if we focus on keeping our communication professional and straightforward, rather than trying to convince people of the righteousness of our personal convictions. Your dreams are yours, and nobody else's. No matter how badly you may want to see someone else approve of your dreams, their approval is never going to make the realization of the goal any sweeter. Just as you assessed your life goals at the beginning of this process to determine what is truly going to make you happy, satisfied, and fulfilled, you must remember now that it was never your friends' approval that filled that need. More importantly, now that you have identified concrete goals that will enhance your quality of life and overall happiness can you honestly say that a friend who would prevent you from reaching them is acting in your best interest?

The people in your life who will unwittingly hinder your progress are, thankfully, much easier to deal with. Sometimes we just haven't done a good enough job of explaining what it is we're after, and so our friends and family misunderstand us. Sometimes they will disagree with your assessment of your own life now as it is, and therefore find themselves at odds with your conclusions about how to improve it. You say you want to drop everything and move to Florida, and they say 'but you love the snow!' Well, that may be true sometimes, but not often enough to keep you out of Florida. We should be thankful that we have these people in our lives because while the misunderstandings can cause some difficulties for us (and them), they love us. The more people you can have on your side to shore up your emotional defenses against a world full of obstacles, fear, and envy, the better the outcome is going to be for the achievement of your dreams, as well as those loving relationships.

Lastly, we'll discuss those that fall into the category of naysayers. These aren't necessarily friends and acquaintances, but what we like to call gatekeepers. These are people who, from their point of view, hold the keys to your success. It is vitally important not to fall into the trap of believing them because there is great folly in their logic.

The gatekeeper can take many forms, and fear and ignorance are their primary weapons. A gatekeeper may be the loan officer at your local credit union, the Dean of admissions at the university, the high-ranking hiring officer at that prominent company, or the owner of the art gallery you'll be trying to sell paintings to. These people hold, to the outside world, very powerful positions. Most of them know it. The roles a gatekeeper may play in the pursuit of our dreams are many and varied, and many of them will be helpful, gracious, even offering useful advice and instruction, or giving advantage where they see the need. However, this will not always be the case, and you must be prepared for an encounter with one of these gatekeepers at some point on your journey.

We find ourselves dealing with these individuals when we need something we simply cannot provide on our own. You may want to apply for that prestigious executive position at that advertising agency, but if they refuse, starting your own agency is probably not in the cards. So, what now? How do we overcome what seems to be the impassable figure of a gatekeeper? The first way is tenacity. If you're at all familiar with the insurance industry, you may have heard that many companies maintain a policy of denying all claims initially, out of hand. The idea is, if every claim is met with a denial, it will help filter out the false claims because only the cases with true damages will persist in search of payment. Sometimes, this same policy is applied to other industries, such as lenders. Don't let the first 'no' you receive be the last one. If you have determined to work hard for your dreams, then you can make sure that anybody who stands in your way will have to work even harder to stop you. In short, don't take 'no' for an answer.

There are other methods to deal with ornery gatekeepers. Sometimes you can actually go around and simply make your own door. That art gallery owner that won't show your paintings? Rent a small space for an evening, dispatch some cheap mailers and Internet marketing, and hold your own showing. While the method may not be what you had in mind when you started out, you've actually succeeded in getting your paintings in front of potential buyers.

We mentioned fear and ignorance are the tools gatekeepers use to keep us out of their world, and here is it how it works. Fear of failure and rejection is what makes them seem so formidable. Let's analyze this and see how it holds up to reality. Failure is not ultimately defined by the actions of some gatekeeper, but by us. We are the ones who determine if our goals will succeed or fail because we are the ones who determine if any obstacle, including gatekeepers, will stop us. The idea of our whole dream riding on the decision of another person should show us the error in the logic. It is our dream to chase, and it is ours to lose. Other people can certainly make our path more difficult, but they can't ever stop us completely unless we let them.

As far as rejection goes, this should be quite easy to dismiss on its face with 2 questions: Why would we concern ourselves with the rejection of strangers, and why do we see rejection as a negative in the first place? The rejection of friends and family can sting, but even that isn't enough to overcome a real desire for change in your life. How much more then should we be able to brush off the rejection of strangers and treat it as so much water off our backs? If that gatekeeper is going to go home tonight without once thinking about you and your problems, then why should you spend any precious time dwelling on them? Moreover, rejection is going to come, it is only a matter of from where, and in what form. If we admit from the outset that rejection will be part of the process of achieving our dreams, then we no longer have to see it as a negative to be avoided, but rather a positive step in the right direction. Instead of a setback, we can count each rejection as a step forward. Don't be crestfallen over rejections, but be encouraged, let each new 'no' renew your spirit of enthusiasm as you press on towards the mark, one by one eliminating the wrong paths until in triumph you finally find the open door to success.

"Change One Thing – <u>Know</u> where you are going and <u>when</u> you want to get there!"

Chapter Four: The Last Mile

Now we face what may be our greatest enemy: ourselves. The potential for man to undermine his own happiness is almost limitless. While others may flail away vainly in attempts to thwart our greatest efforts, without even blinking an eye, we are capable of completely destroying the best-laid plans by our own hands. Yes, we often find ourselves in desperate circumstances, belatedly wondering how it came to pass, all the while having no one to blame but ourselves. Truly, if we are the driving force behind our own success, then we must exercise the same influence over our every failure.

The will to succeed can be great in people, to the point of consuming every other capacity of the person, until the final goal becomes an all-encompassing focus, with pure tunnel vision and single-mindedness leading on to the mark ahead. As strong and momentous a thing the human will may be, we are all too capable of pulling out the very foundations we worked so hard to establish. One of the great problems with the remarkable degree of freedom most of us enjoy in this world is, oddly, the freedom. It is too easy for us to lose sight of the goals we've set for ourselves, to get caught up in consumerism, or social problems, or behind in our obligations financially, and end up putting ourselves in a hole that we may never get out of.

The desire to achieve our dreams, if we are going to succeed, must be an ever-present desire, constantly at the forefront of our thoughts. If you are after real, full-time happiness, it is going to take real, full-time effort; there is no shortcut around it. Nothing less than absolute dedication and perseverance is going to suffice if you are going to be successful at anything that matters to you. The will to succeed must manifest itself in everything you do, think, and say. There simply cannot be a time when you relax, kick back, and decide that dream of yours won't matter for a while. If it is ever to truly matter, it must always matter.

Humans are easily deceived, lulled into a false sense of security, sometimes victims of our very own false assurances. Perhaps you're saving up for a vacation, making sure you have enough to cover a trip through Europe after retirement. If you have 5 years left to save before retirement, then saving money should be at the front of your mind for the next 5 years. Sound grueling? It can be, but anything new can become a habit with enough practice. Smoking is pretty difficult for most people at first, but before you know it inhaling poison becomes something they can't do without. We must become *addicted* to our goals, unable to function without contributing to the furtherance of our progress. If saving money is the goal, you can't go out to eat without knowing that money could be in your retirement account instead. You diligently repair and maintain your car, knowing that the cost of having to purchase a replacement would completely throw off all of your plans. When saving is the goal, every cent you spend must be recognized as a potential savings. If this is how you can view your finances, you will find saving money becomes not just easy, but second nature, which is precisely how you will end up being successful; by making success a habit you just can't break.

The last obstacle we must overcome is ourselves, and we are limited only by our desire to succeed. Complacency kills, and it can sneak up on you when you least expect it. This dream of yours is going to take effort, hard work, constant vigilance, and perhaps desperate measures at times. It will also produce many things along the way. It will bring out in you a drive for more, for something better, an earnest desire to improve or perish. You almost certainly will learn things about yourself that you never knew before, some bad, but hopefully most good. You'll likely identify weaknesses, and learn to strengthen those areas through diligence and perseverance. One thing you can be sure to find in this journey, though, is fear. It will come. It may not be when you expect it, or how you expect it, but you should expect it. Fear is part of the growth process, and the sooner you realize it, the sooner you can start coming to terms with how to handle it.

You and Fear

We've already talked about planning our way through the unknowns of our journey in order to alleviate those fears associated with doing something new and different. The fear that accompanies significant changes to our lives is something we can't avoid, but don't have to. Fear doesn't have to be an obstacle for us, it can be a tool we use to our advantage.

We are used to thinking of fear as a primal reaction, a real physical response to dangers in our environment. The 'fight or flight' response we learn about in school is very much alive and well, but this isn't exactly the kind of fear we're talking about here. Chances are you won't actually face immediate physical, bodily harm while pursuing your dream of a home Internet business or early retirement. While the catalyst of the fear we feel may be quite different from a survival situation-type fear, the reaction we feel within in ourselves is very much the same. Fear can invoke a variety of physical responses in our bodies, from elevated heart rate and blood pressure to shallow breathing, sweating, dilated pupils, and a hypersensitive sense of smell. Generally, we face a much less severe form of anxiety when we consider the fears that keep us from achieving our goals. It may only be some sweaty palms and a little uncertainty in our speech, but the results can be disastrous if we allow it to send us into paralysis.

Fear that leads to inactivity is extremely dangerous. In this situation, you've actually stopped moving in the direction of your goals, thus alleviating the fear and sending signals to your body that you've solved the problem, nothing to be afraid of. The problem is, the next time you go to act on your plan you've already shown yourself how to make the hard times easier: by quitting. Now you'll be much more likely to take the easy way out next time, knowing the physical abatement of fear will soon follow. This will, of course, lead to a new, very undesirable habit, of 'curing' your fear of acting by, well, not acting. Hardly a good recipe for success and productivity.

It may be helpful to remember that you are not alone. Fear is a great motivator for all sorts of people, in every walk of life. Many famous singers and musicians claim to still get butterflies before a performance, but it's nothing like when they first started. The first performance will be nerve-racking, high-tension drama. Once the artist has performed dozens or hundreds of times, the fear is still there, the desire and need to perform flawlessly on demand is still present, but now that fear can drive them to a better performance. It drives their practice when they're off the stage and drives their performance when they're on it. Rather than paralyzing a professional, fear, properly handled and understood, will helpfully motivate a professional to strive for the very best in themselves, using and focusing that energy on something positive.

Likewise, many star athletes are nervous before or during a game, but that same fear is a tool they use to achieve their goals. If you've ever seen a major-league baseball pitcher on the mound, you know what a nervous professional looks like. What makes them star athletes, clutch players, pros who can perform when everything is on the line, is how they react to the fear, that nervousness, those butterflies.

Basically, to decide on a dream for your life, a goal that you've never dared set before, and then pursue it with your entire being, your every effort and full capacity, is going to take courage. Courage is required for greatness; the two simply go hand-in-hand. Courage is not, however, the absence of fear. Heroes are all around us, doing heroic things every day, in small, unnoticeable ways, and in dramatic, extravagant ways, but they all have fear. They have it, they feel it, and they use it. Courage is not the absence of fear, but the ability to act in the face of it. Those who truly have no fear are not brave; they are fools. Or crazy. The brave are those who stand in the presence of fear and let it wash over them, embracing it as part of the process and moving forward anyway, acknowledging that nothing worthwhile will ever come their way without it.

The fear that wells up inside of us at that big moment, right when the money is on the line, and everything is riding on your next move, is there for us to use. We cannot rationalize away fear, we can't eradicate fear, or pretend it away, but we can use it. If we come to see that fear, that unsettled stomach, that nervous uneasiness within us, as a side effect of progress, we will actually come to crave it. That fear will become something you long for, something you seek out and embrace when you find it because to you, it will now mean progress, movement, and one step closer to your dreams. Rather than seeing fear as a sign that you are doing something you shouldn't, it will now be a clarion call to signify success, a declaration of doing the right thing to accomplish great things.

"Change One Thing – <u>Critique</u> your plan on where you want to go and when. It's getting real!"

Conclusion

You've come a long way. When we started, the dream wasn't even real yet. You probably hadn't even said it out loud yet. But now you're here. There is a plan in place, a concrete, actionable plan that will lead you toward the goals you've always wanted to accomplish. You've done the work to lay out a path that when followed, will one step at a time find you arriving at the doorstep of your dreams. Congratulations.

But wait, you're not finished yet. There is one more thing to add to the list, one more step to truly master the process of achieving life-changing goals: evaluation.

We've all likely had jobs where raises and promotions are few and hard to come by. In these kinds of jobs, the system usually employed to designate which employees merit such accolades is a schedule of performance reviews. That wonderful feeling when you sit in your supervisor's office, nervously awaiting his review of your work for the last 6 months or so, hoping to be given some small token of appreciation for all the time and effort you've put in. Now, after all the planning, after all the work, after all the dedication and soul-searching, you've finally arrived at your goal, you've reached the end of your path. Or have you?

This is the moment when, after some celebration, of course, you get to carry out your own performance review. That's right; because when it comes to your life, your goals, your dreams, and especially your happiness, you are your own boss. There is no one else you're ever going to answer to for your happiness. Now you must take the time to calmly and carefully evaluate not just your performance in getting here, but the destination itself.

First, appreciate where you've come from. This was never going to be an easy task, or it wouldn't have taken so much effort and planning. The time and sweat and commitment required to make this journey were worth it, and therefore has a real and tangible value, and you produced it. You are a valuable person who has contributed real value to your own life, and in the process added to the overall quality and enjoyment, you experience in this world. That, my friend, is a big deal.

Second, take the time to evaluate where you are. Some goals we may set for ourselves are big, but don't take a very long time at all, maybe a year or two. Some may take a decade or more. Things change, we learned that on the way here, but things didn't stop changing because we crossed something off the list. Take a deep breath and evaluate how you feel today about the goal you set at the beginning of this process, maybe many years ago. You may have gotten married and had kids, moved for a job or some other reason, all kinds of changes have probably happened in your life since you started this journey, and hopefully all for the better. Now that you have the benefit of hindsight in evaluating the goals you set for yourself be sure that you are now where you thought you were going to be, as well as where you still want to be.

Don't be afraid to decide there may be something different you desire or need, now that you're here. After all, you've made some significant changes already to get where you are, and now you know nothing is stopping you from doing it again.

"Change One Thing – <u>Don't let fear</u> hold you back from starting the journey that is meant to be yours!"

Thank you for reading to the end of the book – R & R

Please leave feedback for this book on Amazon – Cheers – Ray & Ruby